I just want two more Michigan summers

Library of Congress Control Number: 2023917461

United States Copyright Office Registration Number: TXu 2-393-046

First Edition Printing, 2024

Photography by Ayla Batton Wyman
Book Design by David Provolo

ISBN: 979-8-9876216-5-3 (hardcover)
ISBN: 979-8-9876216-3-9 (paperback)
ISBN: 979-8-9876216-4-6 (ebook)

Printed by Small Circle, LLC.
Three Oaks, MI
www.mabwyman.com

malkam@mabwyman.com

For Ayla and Auren, who have made me feel complete…

I just want two more Michigan summers

A COLLECTION OF POEMS

M.A.B. Wyman

Small Circle, LLC
Three Oaks, Michigan
Published 2024, First Edition

Ares

On that day we made a trek across a plain of dirt from a sleek tall thing that landed alone in a red canyon.

"Have you ever been to Mars?" the voices asked.

"No, not at all," we answered.

"Then welcome to our sands," they said.

So we sat and cried and rubbed the grime of forgotten memories and buried friends and loving grandparents into our eyes until there was nothing left but the signs of the universe.

goodbye, my sometime darling...

the sidewalk loves me,
        she knows the sidewalk loves me,

my feet tread slowly, intentionally,
        late at night when   her appeal has gone

i smoke a cigarette on the way home,
        the sidewalk swallows my footsteps

until there's nothing left but
        the sound of my shadow on the concrete.

Nausea in kin to the kind of man I am

In the lonely, lonely night
her hips are sweet as nectarines,
wide and perfumed as the scent
of old dauphines.

These are the summer clippings
in the alcove of my repose,
flowering in the evenings,
like primrose.

She used me and said goodbye, goodbye.

That poor, poor boy tosses
a grapefruit through the window
caught in the grip of madness,
he can see my shadow down below.

Every day, I'm peeling my skin,
in pieces of tawny leather
for my page, my pen,
and then, for all my pleasure.

Every leaf is a sour piece, a sour piece of me.

I confess, "I'm afraid, I'm afraid,
of breaking my fingers at midnight,
on the eve of her retrograde,
before the great sacrifice."

The chants can be heard rising
from the garden of the lost
a great spell galvanizing,
twelve swords uncrossed.

"I won't be coming back from the edge tonight,"
I say, I say.

swimming, in a way...

the fish in my dreams shimmer like polished pennies,
  the river is wide,

      wide,

  the color of the sun,
or a reflection   thereof

they say every passing moment is a story
  for the state of things

      within the world,

  for me, drifting,
circling,   not touching

their scales are like soft glass brushing my neck,
  while I float

      in a flare of fire

  across the wide,
wide,   alone in the river of the sun

the story, the play, the film...

hold on now, my love
> you're not a deep press, steam clean,
>> you can't just jumpstart me like that.

i'm wearing
> this wonderful ice cream suit,
>> but it's due back in fifteen minutes.

come on now,

> don't be like that,

>> i'm still the same man without it,

>>> just not as well dressed, of course,

>>>> but still the same man.

Together

At the end of the evening, our intentions kept us warm, in the wake of a well-earned tragedy.

"Today really sucked," she said; her voice was bitter, stale, and dry, and we wiped our breath upon each other and counted the hours.

A gale swept through, and our hearts were carried out the open window,

> our histories,

> our carriages,

> our unyielding.

And so, we buried our heads and waited to see who would be the first to crawl away.

in the rigors of a three day rain...

he opened a window, overwhelmed
by the autumn odor of dead deer,
      its hooves crushed like walnut shells

in day one, he smoked sweet cigarettes,
thinking about his blood circling the sewer,
      wary of the way down

in day two, during the flood, his tongue swelled,
paralyzed with what he wanted to say,
      he wrote a letter instead

in day three, the final stroke of the storm,
it rained honey & rosewater
      until nightfall

it was the one thing he had ever done
with figurative mastery

The ritual of moldy cheese and bread and sitting

I happened upon a mouse. It was a quivering lonely thing, small as a marble with its tail wrapped around itself like thread – almost as if to keep warm despite the day's blistering sun. The mouse shifted to reveal the vertical gash, the matted fur, greasy with blood and infection. 'It's showing me it's going to die,' I thought. Briefly, I entertained the notion of running for a shoebox, of disinfecting the wounds, of giving this mouse a fighting chance. Then, as if to say, 'Don't bother!' it stiffened, lay over, and died. In that moment, I was heartbroken. After that, I could see the whittling down of the hours of our lives, getting one day closer to death. This mouse and I were the same. We were part of each other. I sat over it. I blessed it with the breath of tobacco. I was then the mouse in pain. I was then the mouse about to die.

Her eyes are blue like October water

She is the spirit of the lake
    on the edge of enlightenment,

Waves crest without rhythm,
    her tempers changing by the strength of the wind.

Her body is fulsome, and rare,
    and I say, "Your beauty is a mirror for this place."

The way is winding and steep,
    and I say, "These dunes are like the curve
    of your hips."

So entwined with my idea of her,
    I say, "You and this place are the same in
    my mind."

Every step is a challenge,
    climbing to the pinnacle
        past the dogwood trees,
            on the mount where the lake fills
            the horizon.

"Yes," she replies, offering a soft kiss,

    the autumn forests, the rolling dunes,

      the shimmering waters,

        caught in every movement, in every

          element

            of her expression.

We go back down the trail together,

    where she points to a herd of deer

      running on the distant hills,

        and we climb over the fallen trees

         in the deep woods.

i just want two more michigan summers

fresh wrought dreams
dangle by a wire, conducting light by glass

sprites bounce through the grove,
full figured & flowery, they greet weary travelers at the door

artisan hands make good work,
shaping clay & goats milk – melting & pouring – twisting & tying
the wicks of our lives

what can be said
of the manufacture of truth beyond the glass edge of tomorrow

coming to life
in kettles & drums, waiting to flow freely back into the earth,

we want what once was,
biding our time, in orchards of light, where beauty sways
& hungers do rise

Sunset Haiku

The evening gathers,
while sparrows and thrushes flit
through the neighborhood.

Tall oak trees in bloom
lit by the sun's final rays,
breaking the west sky.

Red cherry blossoms
swirl to the ground in the breeze,
rolling through the dusk.

The logic of bones and her daily tardiness...

She taught me that our shadows are always bound to our feet, crying, and licking my eyelids after the sun goes down.

The ravens descend like a loud black cloud, telling murder stories, dancing to the tune of war.

She says, "Listen! Listen to the gods," fearless against the wind and rain, naked beneath a veil.

We build fires and throw bones to learn the truth, offering a prick of blood under the moon.

In the hall of kings, there is a sheer opulence
        that tells of revolution, and the death of a monarchy.

Unraveling myself...

The afternoon lists through, and hours of boredom pass. My
hands are forthright, but every task I begin is left incomplete.

In a garden of delight, the libations pour freely and travelers
find respite from the road, but once again the heat of the
candle burns my brow.

Deeply passionate, my efforts are always in vain, the work of
the future lost to an ether of discontent, my present mood.

I have been weary for days, racing through, my hands swell
with intent and my bones wash themselves.

Too often do bleak hearts make shadows on my dreams, too often
do good friends lose their love and followers lose their faith.

Ready is the morning in summer sunlight – yet my heart falls
short of its expectations, weary and restless, I have been, for days.

Muse

Her eyes are a shifting blue – like so many tones in a lakeshore sky.

Threads of fate bind us together. Her beauty inspires scenes of another time – in the land of tomorrow – when we blend our forms – at the dawn of love.

Waves of action define her. Words of truth fall from her lips.

Window at Midnight

Steady rain comes down
to saturate the earth in spring.

Storm clouds hang low all day,
and the north is an ominous sheet of gray.

The horn of the train calls through the night,
while thunder peals
over a field of shadows,
        grown out of the winds of iniquity.

My thoughts are unchained,
running wildly beyond my dreams.

Lightning splits the balance of the night,
cutting like a knife through a shroud.

The train squeals by at the crossing,
fading away
after the thunder has died,
        and only the steady rain comes down.

prayer

there is one truth,
that the beginning of the end is coming

tomorrow,
i don't care what happens,

torn & bruised,
it would be better than living yesterday

can a good mystery
really quench my desire for god?

when i grab that wire,
it sends me a shock to wake me up from a dream

where heaven says,
'yes, death can be defeated, wishes do come true'

since the words that fall
beneath your chin begin to absolve me completely

The Touch of Abraxas

Three girls wait; laughing while one is pierced through the nipple in the hidden caves beneath the street.

There is a tall woman at the door – chosen by the gods – who holds herself ready with a sword to negotiate for the touch of Abraxas.

The stairs spiral down into the catacombs and a row of artists hunch over their work

    of artificery,

        of runecasting,

            of steel needles and springs,

                of painting skin in the sheer light.

They whisper songs in the old language while they imprint warriors,

    and mages,

        and muses alike,

            they see colors

                that cannot be seen.

Coins are traded for the service and behind a glass veil there is a prick of blood,

    where a soldier

        endures the pain,

            and young men flaunt

                their brash enchantments.

In the afternoon, more ladies arrive for charms of flowers and crystals and gems and the phases of the moon.

When it is done, I rise into the streets of the ancient city with a spell of travel on my leg.

silent hunger

the red sun is like a bloody plum,
and from where I sit, the sky is drenched
with its colors

it fades over the belt of the horizon,
and my spirit is woven with the currents
of infinity

cicadas rattle in autumn
and my thoughts rest on the central channel,
while I watch

the blood plum sun

October

Warm autumn winds brush my cheek,
though the sky is threatening rain.

Trees sway their tips, like giants
rubbing shoulders, speaking another language,

the forest is cast in gold,
fading green filigree, inlaid with scarlet.

Each season brings its chores,
and there is much work to be done before the end of the year,

since the ground is littered
with their withering crowns, falling all over me.

Packaging

That day's bottling run is arduous, and after six months I no longer enjoy the novelty of throwing glass on the line.

Within the production room, someone is brewing beer and five men are packaging until time and space have no meaning.

Cigarettes are modern man's runes. We can see our futures in those small cylinders. Each draw is a puff of cancer, intangible and relentless.

Our streams are cast in the wind as quickly as they appear – burning until the ember eats the insignia of the makers of death.

The beer in my mug is hoppy and bitter. My breath is hot with smoke. My hips flare noisily after working all day.

Embarking from home...

The first rituals
are done, and canals spread like twelve fingers from the bay.

She stands before him,
his navigator on a rail, through the long grasses and wildflower fields.

They communicate
with glances and signs, sharing the wisdom of two minds as one.

His wrist tightens down
on the brush, while two women stroll beside green cypresses in the sun.

His hands are the tools
that capture the willful erratic sea, the hoary clouds, the sand in the paint.

They had crossed three lands
to arrive there, where complementary colors don't blend, without request.

An old man blinks twice
against the sleepy rhythm of the train headed west, embarking for home.

summoning

i built up a fire to its peak

it is consecrated
by the blood of a rabbit
the shed of a snake

enclosed in a ring of rune & lore

my prosody wanes
while cicadas sing for love
dogs roam the woods

steel forged by man with heat holds my interest tonight

i am channeling
down an iron spike
the kiss of fire

burns my forefinger white & numb

it is a message
of good tidings
for our quest

by the auspices of the day & the shifts of the earth

gathering his will
the mage opens a gate
to send us abroad together

the bull elephant prepares for a long journey while bright
flames lick three skulls

Gone tomorrow...

Our lives are mere moments
from the threshold of space
beneath the distant torches of the gods.

Time changes the land,
tribes become civilizations, great eras unfold,
the years are as momentary as a sound.

The running of humanity
is like a forest fire, with only enough fuel
to burn brighter or burn longer.

There are many unknowns,
unmarked constants, as infinite as the blades of grass,
or grains of sand

by the shore.

He had me carry it all that way...

I spent some time lying facedown, bleeding out more than in,
the world on my back, shouting, 'just say when, say when,'
the plows splitting me open in the icy road,
the world shouting, 'let's get loaded, get a load.'

I just rolled it up to see what taste it tasted like.

I dug myself a rocket pit, six feet deep, two and a half feet wide,
I took off and it clattered and clanged the whole space ride.
I was up so far I couldn't come back down,
afraid of my old life in that old town.

I went and chewed it up to see what taste it tasted like.

He had me going east when I wanted to go far out west,
he spun me the wrong way, too high in the sky at my request.
Ten shots away from death, he laughs, 'isn't it so unfair?'
Ten shots through in, way out, somewhere.

I just ate it up to see what taste it tasted like.

the mythology of men...

we become shadows
of what we were   grumbling
under the sounds of our production

our humors are bleak
too many hours unfold   unfilled
despite the joys of our work

we can do nothing
but drink & smoke & gripe & fuss
to soothe the pain of our togetherness

some of us lean to lift   breaking our backs

        or we stagger to move   popping our knees

        our hands are swollen & bruised   constantly

like cocks on patrol
alpha dogs that can't be touched
or tools in the shed   young & old

The Property

In her father's manor
the great room is austere in its nostalgia.

Everything is in its place,
art is on the wall, there are books everywhere.

Maiden grass sways
and oak trees stand stalwart behind the house.

The fire in the hearth,
sings a song, 'Laissez le bon temps rouler!"

Many acres surround us,
the occasional pickup truck rumbles down the road.

"A line of turkeys came across
the front yard today, there's a nest of mating hawks in that tree."

"The driveway is a quarter of a mile long.
All the dogs are buried over there, and that's strawberry hill."

"It's a lot to keep up on," he usually says.

Dream of life...

The starlings flit in the crowns of trees that sway in the wind at night.

Across the stage there are nymphs and gods, sultry and bare,
drawn in graphite and coal.

The largest of us have wasted into apathy, caught in the nets of
avarice, where youth and beauty, love and fear, are torn away.

Only our bones remain, on the line between dreams, forever lost
in the place where we eat our own souls.

the hegemony of me over myself...

here is an explanation
 for why i am the way i am

when i was a boy
a tornado set down in the house,
after heavy rain all day

it came to steal our souls
 came to whip them from our bare skin

devouring us all
until only scraps were left
dangling in the jaws of the wind

now there is a slow fear within me,
 for i am cocooned in the silk of my own self-loathing

I remember when I caught you dreaming...

I stood there in the door, harrowed and weary, the breath of the cigarette idly burning, hardly visible, shapely like a lone fish in a pirouette.

That night was not like other nights; lost in a shuffle of my own noise, hurting by the downy layer of ash upon my heart.

You had honeysuckle in your hair, there was peace in the valley of your dreams, and I could thumb the pages of your poetry attached, like me, to your body.

I remember the moment when the waning light began to chase away the shapes from under your eyelids until they were flimsy to your touch.

Then I witnessed your arousal. You sat up. Coughed. Swept your hair from your face and asked, "What time is it?"

I answered, "Late. You fell asleep."

"Hmm, I was so tired," you said as you reclined.

I remember that I had not wanted to interrupt, but I was glad you were finally awake.

The journey tomorrow...

There are two abbeys behind us, a small city on the horizon,
playing out a fable, the honeybee and the dragonfly, roaming
past whirling giants that pulled power from the sky.

Alleys twist between skinny houses in a medieval village,
boats float idly along the canal and the market is bare at dawn
where bells ring joyously every quarter hour.

We spend the day drinking beer in a high tower,
exploring the historic center, up and down, our feet are pounding
the cobblestones, hungry for waffles and chocolate.

A hidden lane leads to a garden of two lovers on a terrace,
the heart of an ancient place, standing intertwined through time
we are changed, as our spirits have arrived there together.

Our new home is a small reprieve, with hot water to bathe,
food and drink to enjoy, a restful bed, before our journey continues
bright and early, tomorrow morning.

Tapestry

My body is not my own,
every hair and tooth and muscle and bone is a thread to the past,

with the blood of the first ones
pumping in my veins, I am woven with their great ambitions,

pounding with ancestral anger
I unravel my history, reaching back and forth for their sacred wisdom.

My father was rejected
by our society, and his father was just a boy, drafted to fight an unjust war,

the line of tortured fathers
sprawls into history, like lines on a map, train yards, factories, warehouses.

What we have built
is proud, and broken; rational, and repressed, and taken from within ourselves.

How little it means to spread our seed,
when we have caused the blights on our own lands,
the death of our own stewardship.

For what? For greed? For power?
And how far will our actions carry into the future?
A thousand years.

So, in this new era, I am left
to gather strength from the ones who provided
for me to stand here now.

Abbey Rising

We walk over the long salt marshes
where the locals search for mussels, like treasure in the muck.

The causeway stretches for miles
into a point where the abbey rises against the broad cloudless sky.

With the throng we pass under the iron gates,
just as we had done before, our bodies tingling, our faces flush.

I walk with her on the high wall
overlooking the vast black waters that expand to the sea.

Her lips taste like the salt on the wind,
and she holds my hand on the cobbled lane leading up the mount,

into the cathedral, showered with light
from the high windows tucked between the arches, bells tolling
for an empty room.

We climb higher, to the hall of knights,
their tombs graced by ageless flowers, encircled by columns to bear
the weight of heaven.

An angel lands on the summit,
holding his sword aloft, wearing a fiery crown, wings shining
in the midday light.

The way down is faster than the way up,
returning through the old village, back under the gates at dusk.

We hike out on the causeway
past dunes sculpted by the rivers on the right, and flat marshes on the left,

the abbey diminishing into a memory again.

leadership of men...

my thoughts are aflame,
the fruits of my work lost
in the hearth of pride

the men are tired
of my complaints,
of all my demands on a world that turns

but too much has happened,
too much have i endured to lose sight of the end

my body is a forge
flashing red with more heat
than anyone can bear

hardened from work,
their hands are flayed,
their hearts are harrowed & desolate

my words cut to the truth,
because my words are like a hateful knife

Sword

I carry the wind and the wave slung over my back.

Stones gleam on the lakeshore,
the tide rolls, churning down the line.

My hands grip the hilt.

The wind is a constant force,
the wave turns in circles and streams,

every step is etched into the sand.

Forms come together in momentary bliss
dissolving into the ether of time.

Creative measures are taken with the blade at practice.

In autumn, the dune grass has faded,
the sky is aflame, navy and charcoal.

Meridians open, the first step on the path to the void.

The lake shimmers, reflecting the sky,
they merge into the horizon.

The practice becomes a rhythm, which becomes harmony.

When the forms are complete
I carry the wind and the wave across my back,

where it waits to be used again.

in the land of the early risers...

as the roots grow
the field speaks
in riddles of the harvest

cicadas bloom after a long sleep
dogs bay in their kennels for the scent of pheasants on the wing
the foreman's truck kicks up plumes of dust on a dirt road

the fields are wet with dew
soil clings around the wrist
the grapes are ripe on the vine

a hawk circles overhead in sight of a vole for lunch
the crops are harvested, farmers clear their lands before winter
the day begins before the sun has risen & it never ends

Nighttime Sojourn

In the floodlight, a moth twists its shadow over me, and I am
dazzled by the lack of geometry in my trails of smoke.

A low rising half moon is dressed in the silk of drifting clouds,
and the night's worries come in dry currents of summer wind.

I can barely hold my heart's fire, the stars swell in my eyes;
the road yearns for my feet across its back.

The buzzing rhythms of cicadas join the songs of tree frogs and
crickets rubbing their legs, filling my ears with their endless poetry.

I stand alone in a meadow under the light of the sky, I stand as
still as a lonely tree until I am dissolved into the night.

Greenbush 2016

The beer stink has soaked into my boots, and we sit in defeat, reminding each other nothing can be done about the past.

She tries to tell me, "It's because you are a sharp tool, like a sword. People have to be careful when they handle you."

It is true, I am made of impure materials, tempered by the heat of the forge, sharpened and honed, dangerous and glistening.

Always ready to be used, always ready to cut down whatever is ahead; but my early moves betray too much longing and intent.

She says, "Only someone who is trained will know how to use you," since; after all, the sword is a weapon of esteem, a tool for a scholar.

It must be handled with skill, and finesse, and with the strength of conviction, otherwise the blade will cut back.

When you write, just tell the truth...

My pages flutter in the wind behind the annex, and the head of my beer is a delicate, fragrant, lace.

I try to wait; for inspiration, for my newest friend to arrive, for pages to fill themselves – running my poetry to the margins.

"I heard you were a writer," he says, although I'm not even sure what that means, since he seems to be telling me to give up.

The night is bright, cloudless and surreal with the energy of humans buzzing on the libations of their choice, hollering in the streets.

"There's a million of them and only one of you," my friend declares, the smoke filling his mouth, the smooth ale exciting his proud humor.

"Then it's no wonder that I have to be the one to change," I tell him while my spirit collapses into itself. "It's not fair!"

Yet, as I've been taught, a little goes a long way, and the tighter I can be, the smaller my spirit can become, the closer to the truth I can go.

Père Lachaise

Graves and mausoleums line the cobbled lanes. Some are lavish
stone houses; great expressions of wealth on a hilltop, and
others are tombs overgrown with bramble and green lichen,
indecipherable. Golden leaves crunch under our feet as we
walk. There are scattered visitors. An old woman sweeps off
her beloved's grave, and groups gather to pay tribute to the
famous dead. The narrow lanes twist without reason through
the trees, crossing at odd junctions, ending at strange points.
This place harbors the bodies of artists and philosophers and
poets who have changed the world, and we walk for hours,
cutting between headstones and monuments until we stand at
the highest point overlooking the field of bones. Here is the
end of thought; the end of passion; the end of the heart, and
the end of the wild potential of young people who burned out
their own brief lights before they could fade away. We stay and
view their graves, as they would have wished us to do. Then we
trudge downhill and let the streets envelop us again. Somber
thoughts follow like shadows to the river, and we ride the water
taxi until the cemetery is miles away and the bustle of the
city is oblivious to the state of our hearts. The arc of triumph
beckons us down the strip until we are thoroughly exhausted,
and cheated, and amazed by all our human achievements.
How long will we be in love? How long will time give us to be
together? How long is the sunrise of our lives? By the end of
the night we walk beside a tower of light, hearing the plangent
sound of the crow.

My Path

The winter winds speak through the trees until their whispers
become a roar, twisting their tips together.

So often the words are lost, even when the message is hurtling
across the land, just waiting to be heard.

We sit captivated by the waning of the moon and the seasons
of the earth, and the tides that have always rolled.

We now see that we have created the walls that stand in our own way,
imposing ourselves over the mysteries that have long eluded us.

The flow of these things are only broken by trying to understand them.
There are no bridges or tunnels or hidden shortcuts.

We can only sleep with the land and be carried by the sea;
we can only ride the wind and get lost in the fire.

We can only walk the path.

the end is a new beginning...

we are taken to the air
where shelves of cloud obscure the world
breaking over the sea

by tomorrow we return
to the work of alchemy, in our home
with our menagerie

the only sadness we might have
is the unfulfilled moments, of when we are not together,
of the memory that is a dream

the planes call in their orbits,
moving into alignment for a greater purpose
pulling us to their gates

She did...

She sat down one day to write a poem.

She sat down one day to say, "I can feel the breath of the earth. The movements are eager and joyful, final and tragic, wrought in sunlight."

So, he releases the chains of the past and rises up in love, and by the end of the song she has her clothes off.

She says, "Music is such a gift. Music is such a gift."

Coffee Shop

This place is liberating and wild,
polite and courteous, a funny city,
full of cheerful traffic.

We walk on the east side by the bay,
through markets of leather goods, trinkets
and curios, street foods, elixirs, and drugs.

The women ride by, upright in their seats,
hair flowing behind them, gone in a second,
like a thousand other people.

Ten boys play soccer in the alley
riding bikes and prowling the bars,
bored with the pleasures of their old town.

The canals ripple with tugboats,
and gondolas carrying lovers on a cruise
make black waves that break against the bricks.

The streets are always busy
with throngs of people on the sidewalk,
and the occasional gusts of hard, sweet, decadent smoke.

We spend our last afternoon
watching the sun drop behind baroque
houses, their copper spires glistening in the distance.

No Teacher

I am cut from my feet and thrown to the ground.

There is a moment of awakening from the force – standing
up quickly, ready to fight – my new philosophy resounds,
This is all bullshit!

Because aren't we all just standing in a room practicing what
some old man has claimed to be the fundamental truth?
Aren't we all just puppets for our teachers?

Knowledge is power? More like knowledge is bullshit! When all
things are known, then nothing is from the heart.

Questions are asked; harsh words are given in response. It
becomes apparent that beyond knowledge, beyond truth,
there is only personal respect.

Later, the master says, 'You are in the shadow of a fool, but the
solution is simple, just discover yourself, and make it your own.'

Seek the joy of alignment and form; then you will find meaning
where none exists.

Wayward

He says, "It's going to be a cicada summer," as we follow him
through the back valley, tripping into a memory – voices on
the wind – that light cutting the sky.

The trough is a frozen haven in the shoulders of the dune –
tracks are fresh from a bunch of deer running, bold imprints
in the sand and snow.

We climb together to unfathomable heights, collapsing into
each other's arms, our dreams on our tongues.

Shifting coils of color and light – roots as deep as the crown –
sentences writing themselves – in the land past the ethereal veil.

I ask her, "Is it time to let that painting go?"

"Yeah, it probably is," she answers, and she knows it will be
like giving up one of the greater moments in life, unrealized,
misunderstood.

Like wayward travelers following a trickster astray in the valley
of the sleeping giants, lost in the memory of tomorrow.

In a cloud, in a wall, in a chair...

The chill winter wind steals the smoke from my lips,
when the cards are pulled, and the fates set down their favors,
all thoughts of love and the taste of wheat and the rolling
of time disappear.

I wish I could see the hidden movements
of the makers of craft, the dancing trouble, the lion pacing away,
but even with unlimited knowledge at my fingertips,
I fail to understand.

My childhood is gone, the barest reverie of nostalgia;
my years as a young man are gone, like lessons of regret, horizons
yet unexplored; so what can I do now but speak the truth
and seek the truth?

A single man strides purposefully down the road,
green pastures and clouds drift like blossoms on the wind;
how did they buy into his brand of madness? Was he prophet?
Or a poet?

Waiting in Time

They are made of old junk – pieces of pipe welded into a form –
a hero stripped away.

Surrounded by history in the grand stairwell – impressed by
lances of light falling down.

They are a raw being – standing against uncertainty – upright,
indomitable.

Cast in bronze – grim and austere – one side of his face is molten,
scarred by the sun.

Retreating from the accidental – in search of what is essential –
the universal rhythm.

He is neither perfect nor imperfect – glimmering like a torch –
nothing too much.

She is a beauty from ancient days – counterpoised and sensual –
drawing out the faithful.

Imagine her set among the verdant trees, grape vines heavy with fruit – sultry and bare.

Now her arms are gone – her head shorn from her neck – her supple curves worn away.

Carven lions cast in bronze – chiseled arches – marble staircases and massive galleries.

Mythic figures of light and beauty – made of hard stone, flashes of fire – from the heart.

All worked by hands that became dust – hands that only the sculpture can remember.

running all night...

bones on the shelf,
      are dry like oak leaves in the street,
          & redundant shame

now we are against the current,
      irreverent – like dogs that run away from home,
          chasing some hidden truth

it is a time for crossings,
      when winds collide, for love, for possibility,
          existing just for a moment,

we run all night to the end of our lives

Weko

Opposing energy saturates the earth,
waves rolling over themselves create a dull, crashing, whisper.

Clouds hang like shades over the lake,
heavy with rain in spring, reflecting my mood, leaden with grief.

Long grasses flutter on the foredune,
leaves quake on the branches of trees touched by the wind.

The essence of the spirit is limitless
in the air and earth and water, in the positive and negative.

Sunbeams descend like golden arrows,
and the curve of the shoreline is a mutable blue in the distance.

My spirit rises into the veil of infinity,
searching for a vision of another place, a day – an hour – in
    another life.

The Mothership

She's in bad need of a tune up, an oil change, a new fuel filter,
a rebuilt carburetor, and the tranny plug fell out miles ago.

Together we ride her north to the mystical bridge, and further
to the old growth woods with the dogs piled in and the gear
all stowed.

Strange sounds lead to other realms – amber waters crashing
down – descending in layers along the river, noisy all through
the evening.

Darkness saturates – waves of blue lights hatch out of the trees –
strange stories appear to change their rhythms.

She's just running on dreams, blissful hopes for the future,
wheels on the ground and ten gallons of gas in the tank,
all the way to the edge.

Two Masters

Old men debate the stances – the language of the body – the alignment of twelve meridians.

There is a subtle confusion between the followers. Who do we trust? The renowned visitor? Or the esteemed elder?

They were both taught by the same man, years ago, a thousand miles away, the last of a traditional lineage.

Students with questions are a challenge and must be put in their place; long held customs are broken into mere mysteries.

Too many times have we been misled in search of the truth behind the form, waving our hands like clouds, hearts full of fire.

It is a long talk on our sit bones, legs crossed, in honor of two masters – one man is sick, with a legacy, telling stories that slip away.

"Okay, okay, I will explain," the other man says, teaching the magic – the power of thought – the importance of belief.

By the end the masters hold hands and declare they are brothers – our two schools are now one – grasping at shards.

Sundown Theater

Trapped by the melody of the night, suffering booze and grass
after the waning quarter moon, my exuberance rises like embers
over the fire, happily setting the scene for mischief.

Tales of enchantment fall from her lips, a script of words that
invoke spells wrought for romance and nights dressed as
hobgoblins, kings and queens, and lovers lost in the woods.

All the characters step into place, tied to the plot, and soon
the end is just as powerful as the beginning.

magemonk

he knows
great immortals
roam the world,
shapeless,   relentless & passionate,
   whimsical & dangerous

his tools
are nearby,
a wizard's tome
open on the lectern,   to the critical page,
   reading an ancient prayer

two mirrors
transept time,
conjoining reality
through henges & rings, tongues of fire   scorching
   careless hands

in that room
art & physics
have no meaning,
blood from the wrist,   blood in the current,
   blood for a sacrifice

vast farmlands,

oceans & forests,

cities & suburbs,

all vast illusions,   pieces of ash,

   broken glass & rims of steel

deep caverns

reveal scenes

from the old world

of hunters in a dance,   of mythical beasts,

   of a sea of reaching hands

brewing under the half moon

grains steeped in hot water make for sweet runoff,
saving the specialty malts for last,

steel balances on the hearthstone,
where columns of steam rise out of copper kettles

from one thing to another, we are making liquid gold,
combining every element,

precisely to the minute,
enzymes denaturing, proteins precipitating

the oils of jasmine & orange roll between our fingers,
the taste of honey on our lips,

so in the life of a brewery,
alchemical flashes half full & gas escapes like a fragrant flower

Endless...

There are ten thousand pages already written, and I seek to add my own to be lost in the oeuvre of human creation.

We see how momentary art can be, consumed in mass quantities, there are really only a few now that will have any legacy beyond the year they sold best.

The mad dashes of paint and the erratic sounds of music and the pursuit of beauty and truth through verse are part of the old world now.

I wonder what inspiration I can create that might last after I am dead, but I know this journal is filled with ideas, and prose, that will never be found.

Five-Year Anniversary Poem

Time stands still when we are together, but the days slip away into our memories.

Long ago, in another life, I asked you to wear my ribbon around your wrist.

We tied ourselves together and jumped off that bridge, to arrive here, to find each other, to share everything.

How many times have we made a new life for ourselves? Started over again?

You make me whole. Your lips soothe my heart. Your touch heals my wounds.

Everyday you point at something beautiful for me to see. Sometimes we cry, but always we laugh.

We are as old as the earth. We are trees entwined at the roots.

We are a pair of mating cardinals nesting in a honeysuckle tree every year.

Part of me feels lucky, but the other part knows we have always been together, all through time.

You are what I always hoped I would find, and what I never knew I wanted.

Auren Dale

You are the high mountain valley
where we conceived of you,
just as a thought, then as a word, then as a thing.

You are a new flower,
growing tall and strong and beautiful,
from your mother's body, from the earth, from the garden.

You will bloom one day for us,
turning your head to the sound and the sight
of my voice in the sky, to the clouds, to the summer sun.

You are the link to the past; you are our message to the future.

You are a mewling bird,
shrieking like the red tailed hawk
that just moved into the neighborhood.

Author's Note

I originally began to explore poetry as a young man in college,
mostly to improve my skills as a fiction writer. I had always set
out to be a novelist, and while I really enjoy reading poetry,
I always felt that I was missing something essential in order
to be fully realized as a poet.

So, I studied the classics in literature. I learned the rules of
prosody; I devoured the old forms of sonnets and sestinas and
haiku; and I did plenty of free writing in my journal, but for
a long time I denied that I was actually a poet. I focused on
fantasy and science fiction, which offer a vision of another time
and place where the world could be different, perhaps better,
where all things are possible, and nothing is ever lost.

But, poetry conveys something internal. Like other arts, poetry
is subjectively good or bad. It is either meaningful or meaning-
less. It either speaks to you, and opens up its message within
your mind, or it doesn't, and that is nobody's fault. I came to
feel that poetry ought to be more than just playful usages of
words and images. It ought to speak from my inner self to your
inner self, and after that there should then be a tie of meaning
between us as humans that have all endured essentially the
same pains, the same joys, the same difficulties in our lives.

So...I wrote a chapbook. I wanted to explore the freedoms, and the constraints, of poetry on my own terms. Perhaps my message will be too subtle, or maybe it will hit you over the head, but either way at least the words are out there for people to enjoy, and for me. There is a singular kind of happiness that comes from finishing a project, and from creating a thing for people to consume over and over again, whether it is a lovely sip of beer, or a set of verses ringing with truth in your head.

And now it means that I can move on to the next thing. I can outline another novel. I can devise a new plot, with new characters. I can write the next journal of poetry, because this one is done.

M.A.B. Wyman

Malkam is an aspiring author living in Three Oaks, MI, brewing beer by day and writing novels by night. Born and raised in Kalamazoo, Malkam is proud to be a child of deaf adults (CODA), and a graduate of Western Michigan University with a Bachelor in Fine Arts. He is a dedicated student of martial arts and has studied Taiji and Kung Fu for twenty years. Malkam is an avid reader of literature and poetry, and has been participating in storytelling and performance art with Indigan Storyteller Workshops since 2013.